TinkerActive

WORKBOOKS

PRE-K · ENGLISH LANGUAGE ARTS · AGES 4–5

by Megan Hewes Butler

illustrated by Pat Lewis

educational consulting by Randi House

 Odd Dot · New York

The Alphabet: Letters A to D

With the help of an adult, read the poem. Then follow the instructions in the last line of the poem.

Alphabet Game

Letters, letters in a row.
Read them fast, then read them slow.
Point to each letter as you go!

Now use the alphabet, just the same,
To help you play this little game:
Find the letters that spell your name!

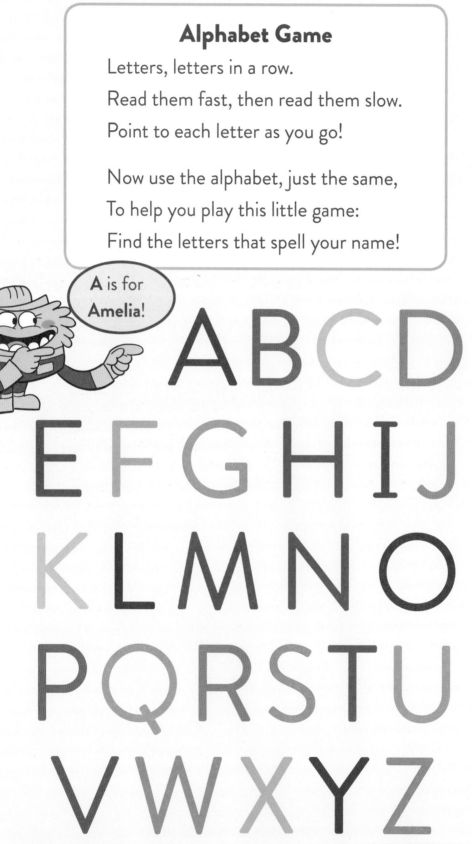

Aa

Trace the uppercase and lowercase letters with your finger. Then trace and write the letters with a pencil. Start a new letter at each dot.

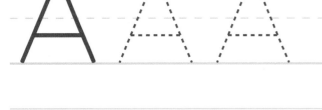

Say it aloud: **Apple** starts with the /a/ sound.
Color all the apples.

Bb

Trace the uppercase and lowercase letters with your finger.

Then trace and write the letters with a pencil. Start a new letter at each dot.

B B B

b b b

Say it aloud: **Ball** starts with the **/b/** sound. Draw a line between the matching letters.

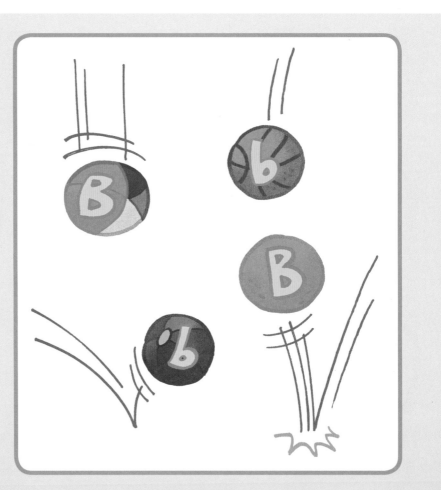

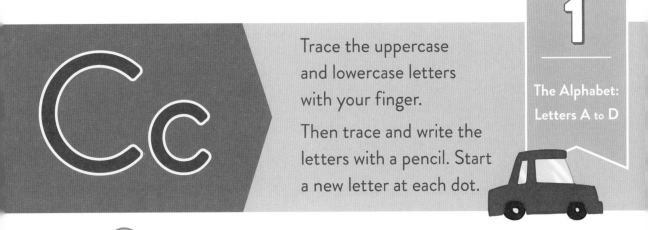

Cc

Trace the uppercase and lowercase letters with your finger.

Then trace and write the letters with a pencil. Start a new letter at each dot.

Say it aloud: **Car** starts with the /c/ sound.

Circle each car with a **C** or **c**.

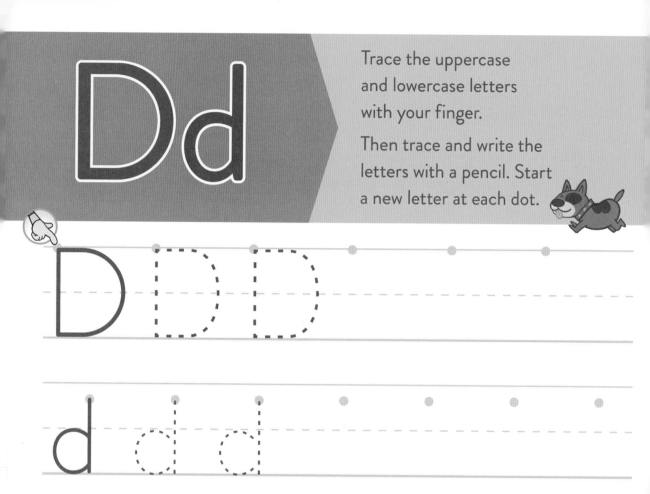

Dd

Trace the uppercase and lowercase letters with your finger.

Then trace and write the letters with a pencil. Start a new letter at each dot.

Say it aloud: **Dog** starts with the **/d/** sound.

Draw a line to lead the dog along the path to his doghouse.

MAIL

Meet the MotMots!

This is Amelia. Her favorite letter is **A**. Circle all the blocks with the letter **A**.

Point to the pictures on the blocks that start with the /a/ sound and say their names aloud.

Plastic garbage bag	Scissors (with an adult's help)	Shaving cream	Glue	3 paper cups
Food coloring	Spoon	Plastic freezer bag	Paper plates	Stapler

LET'S TINKER!

With the help of an adult, **make** a workspace that can get messy by cutting open a garbage bag and laying it flat on a table. **Spray** a pile of shaving cream onto the middle. What does it feel like when you touch it? How does it move when you drag your hands through it? **Rub** it over the garbage bag to make a flat surface and draw in it with your fingers. What letters can you write?

LET'S MAKE: STICKY WINDOW ART!

1. **Squeeze** glue into 3 paper cups, about as deep as your fingertip in each.

2. **Choose** 3 colors and add 1–3 drops of food coloring into each cup. **Mix** each with a spoon.

3. **Lay** a plastic freezer bag on a table and smooth it out so it's flat.

4. **Scoop** some colored glue onto the plastic bag. The spoon can help you move it around to create designs. You can **make** letters, shapes, or other pictures!

5. **Let** your designs dry overnight. Then **peel** them off the plastic and stick them on a window!

LET'S ENGINEER!

The MotMots are having a Letter B Picnic for Brian's birthday! They must each bring foods that start with the letter B. Brian was carrying blackberries, broccoli, bacon, and a bagel, but his plate tore into two pieces!

How can Brian carry his food with a paper plate that is torn in half?

With the help of an adult, **cut** your paper plate in half. Can you use the pieces to carry items? **Try** stacking or bending the pieces. **Try** putting the pieces back together in a new way, like making a basket. **Use** a stapler to hold your design together, and add any necessary materials to make your new object work. Then **find** foods in your own kitchen that start with the letter B and test out your carriers!

PROJECT 1: DONE!
Get your sticker!

The Alphabet: Letters E to H

Trace the uppercase and lowercase letters with your finger.

Then trace and write the letters with a pencil. Start a new letter at each dot.

E E E E

e e e

Say it aloud: **Egg** starts with the **/e/** sound.

Draw a design on each egg.

Ff

Trace the uppercase and lowercase letters with your finger.

Then trace and write the letters with a pencil. Start a new letter at each dot.

F   F   F   F

f   f   f   f

Say it aloud: **Fox** starts with the **/f/** sound.

Color all the foxes.

Meet the MotMots!

This is Brian. He loves playing with his pet fish. Start at the dot and trace each line that shows where his pet swam.

Gg

Trace the uppercase and lowercase letters with your finger.

Then trace and write the letters with a pencil. Start a new letter at each dot.

G G G G G G G

g g g g g g g g

Say it aloud: **Goat** starts with the /g/ sound.

Draw a line to lead the goat along the path to the grass.

H h

Trace the uppercase and lowercase letters with your finger.

Then trace and write the letters with a pencil. Start a new letter at each dot.

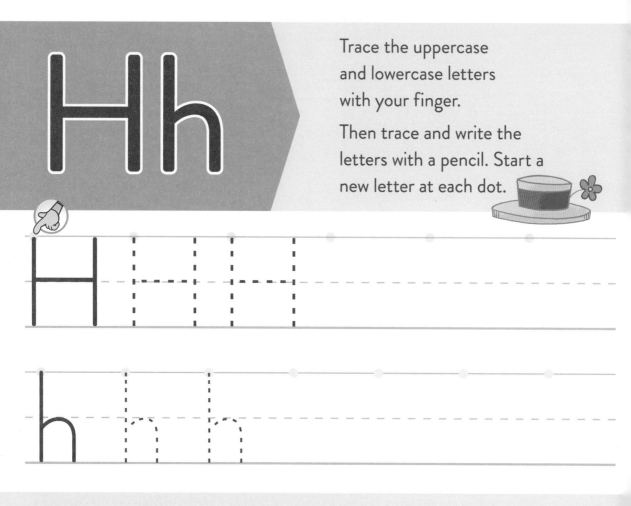

Say it aloud: **Hat** starts with the **/h/** sound.
Color each hat with an **H** or **h**.

Meet the MotMots!

This is Callie. She loves to build paper houses. Start at the dot and trace the path to each house.

LET'S START! GATHER THESE TOOLS AND MATERIALS.

Plastic garbage bag	Scissors (with an adult's help)	Salt	Cotton swab	Flour	Water	1 large bowl and 3 small bowls

Food coloring	Spoon	Paper plate	4 pieces of paper	Crayons or markers	Tape

LET'S TINKER!

With the help of an adult, **make** a workspace that can get messy by cutting open a garbage bag and laying it flat on a table. **Pour** about a cup of salt onto your workspace. **Use** your finger to move it around. **Try** pushing, dragging, and twirling your fingers. Also **try** using a cotton swab. How does the salt move and change? What letters, shapes, and pictures can you make?

LET'S MAKE: MICROWAVE PUFF-UP PAINT!

1. **Mix** 1 cup of flour, 1 cup of water, and 1 teaspoon of salt in a large bowl until there are no clumps.

2. **Pour** the mixture into 3 small bowls. **Add** 1–3 drops of food coloring to each.

3. Use a spoon and a cotton swab to paint letters or shapes on the paper plate. **Try** to apply a thick layer of paint—it will puff up more.

4. Microwave your art for 20–50 seconds to watch it dry and puff up! (Thin paint will cook quickly, while thicker paint needs a bit longer.)

LET'S ENGINEER!

Callie is building a model of Tinker Town out of paper. There should be a house for each MotMot who lives on her street: Amelia, Brian, and herself!

How can Callie show which house belongs to each MotMot?

Build your own paper houses! Then **write** the first letter of each MotMot's name on their house: **A**, **B**, and **C**. **Make** one house yours by writing the first letter of your name on it! What other houses or buildings can you make for Callie's model?

PROJECT 2: DONE!
Get your sticker!

The Alphabet: Letters I to M

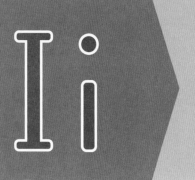

I i

Trace the uppercase and lowercase letters with your finger.

Then trace and write the letters with a pencil. Start a new letter at each dot.

Say it aloud: **Igloo** starts with the **/i/** sound. Color each block with an **I** or **i**.

J j

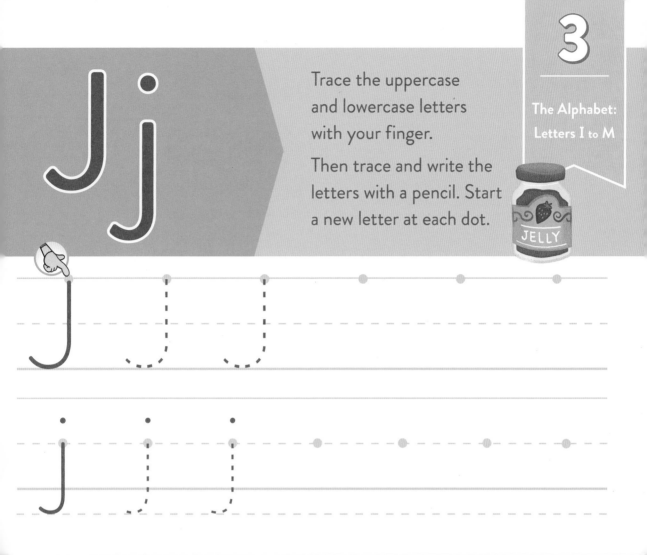

Trace the uppercase and lowercase letters with your finger.

Then trace and write the letters with a pencil. Start a new letter at each dot.

Say it aloud: **Jelly** starts with the **/j/** sound. Draw a line to connect each pair of matching letters.

K k

Trace the uppercase and lowercase letters with your finger.

Then trace and write the letters with a pencil. Start a new letter at each dot.

K K K

k k k

Say it aloud: **Kite** starts with the **/k/** sound.
Color all the kites.

Meet the MotMots!

This is Dimitri. He loves drums. Color each drum that has the letter **D**, like his name.

L l

Trace the uppercase and lowercase letters with your finger.

Then trace and write the letters with a pencil. Start a new letter at each dot.

Say it aloud: **Leaf** starts with the /l/ sound. Say each word aloud. Circle the objects with names that start with the /l/ sound.

Mm

Trace the uppercase and lowercase letters with your finger.

Then trace and write the letters with a pencil. Start a new letter at each dot.

M M M M

m m m m

Say it aloud: **Map** starts with the **/m/** sound.
Draw a line along the path to lead Brian to the map.

LET'S START!

About 1 cup of dried beans	Glue	Piece of construction paper	Baking tray
Salt	Watercolor paint and paintbrush	About 30 mini marshmallows	About 30 toothpicks (with an adult's help)

LET'S TINKER!

Pour your dried beans onto the tray. Can you stack them, roll them, or make them into shapes? **Try** making them into a flat surface and drawing in them. What letters can you draw? **Try** lining them up into rows. What letters can you form?

LET'S MAKE: SPARKLE ART!

1. **Draw** a design on a piece of construction paper with glue. **Add** letters to your design.

2. **Place** your art on a baking tray and sprinkle with salt until the glue is completely covered. **Lift** the paper and shake the excess salt off onto the tray.

3. Let the glue dry overnight.

4. Use a paintbrush and watercolor paint to add color to your sparkly salt designs.

LET'S ENGINEER!

It's snowing in Tinker Town! Dimitri built forts out of snowballs and sticks. Now he wants to build something new.

How can Dimitri use sticks and snowballs to build letters?

Make your own letters with mini marshmallows and toothpicks.
Use the marshmallows to connect the toothpicks.
How can you make straight lines, like the letter **T**?
Can you make curved lines, like the letter **O**?
Can you make the letters in your name?

PROJECT 3: DONE!
Get your sticker!

The Alphabet: Letters N to Q

Nn

Trace the uppercase and lowercase letters with your finger.

Then trace and write the letters with a pencil. Start a new letter at each dot.

N N N N

n n n

Say it aloud: **Nest** starts with the **/n/** sound. Circle each nest.

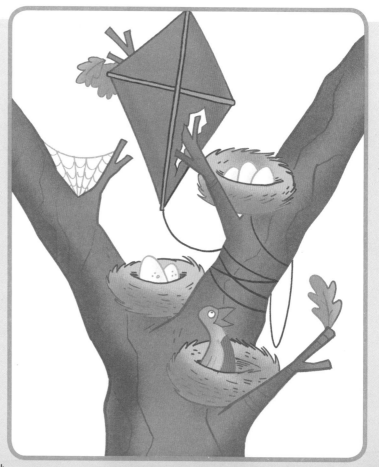

Meet the MotMots!

This is Enid. She loves writing her name. Names begin with capital letters. Trace a capital letter **E** on each of her items.

Trace the uppercase and lowercase letters with your finger.

Then trace and write the letters with a pencil. Start a new letter at each dot.

Say it aloud:
Octopus starts with the **/o/** sound.
Color all the octopuses.

28

P p

Trace the uppercase
and lowercase letters
with your finger.

Then trace and write the
letters with a pencil. Start
a new letter at each dot.

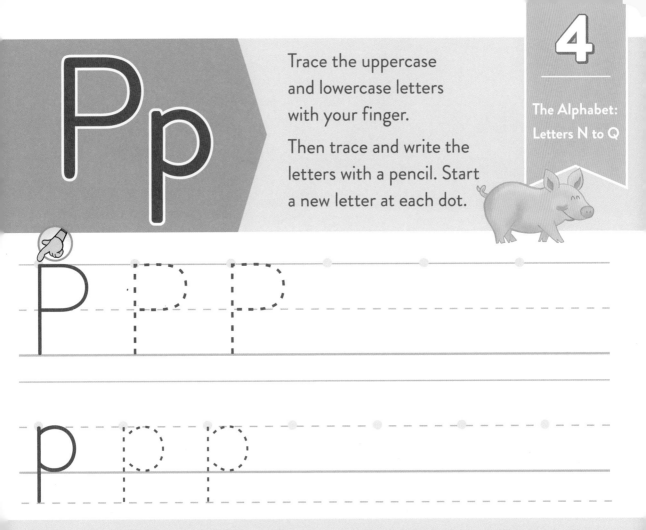

P P P P

p p p p

Say it aloud: **Pig** starts with the **/p/** sound. Say the name of each object
aloud. Circle the objects with names that start with the **/p/** sound.

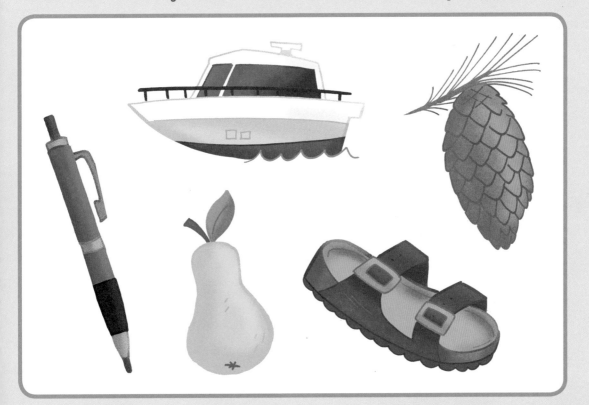

Meet the MotMots!

This is Frank. He loves animals. Trace the missing letters to complete the name of each animal.

do g

pig

cat

fox

Q q

Trace the uppercase and lowercase letters with your finger.

Then trace and write the letters with a pencil. Start a new letter at each dot.

Q O O O

q q q

Say it aloud: **Quilt** starts with the **/qu/** sound.
Draw a line between the matching letters.

LET'S START! GATHER THESE TOOLS AND MATERIALS.

Paper | Pencil | Washable paint | Small bowls | Cotton swabs | Cotton ball

Knife (with an adult's help) | Lemon | Baking tray | 4 or more flat stones | Modeling clay | Permanent marker (with an adult's help)

LET'S TINKER!

Draw lines, shapes, and letters on a piece of paper with a pencil.
Squeeze paint into a small bowl.
Dip a cotton swab into the paint, and make dots on your lines.
Can you make letters with dots?
What happens if you use a cotton ball instead?

LET'S MAKE: SECRET MESSAGES!

1. With the help of an adult, **cut** a lemon in half.

2. Squeeze the juice into a small bowl.

3. Use a cotton swab like a paintbrush to write and draw with the lemon juice on a piece of white paper. You can **write** letters or draw pictures. Your message will be invisible!

4. With the help of an adult, **preheat** an oven and a baking tray to 350 degrees.

Put the message on the baking tray and in the oven for around 3–8 minutes.

5. Watch carefully and remove the tray when you can see your message. It can change quickly!

LET'S ENGINEER!

Frank wants to teach Callie about the alphabet! But he can't find his alphabet blocks.

How can Frank show the letters and their sounds?

Make your own alphabet blocks! **Look** at your paper, stones, and modeling clay. Could any of these materials be used to show letters? How can you make pictures that start with the sound that each letter makes? Can you make an alphabet toy for each letter of your name? You can **use** the letter and picture stickers on page 129 to help.

PROJECT 4: DONE!
Get your sticker!

Rr

Trace the uppercase and lowercase letters with your finger.

Then trace and write the letters with a pencil. Start a new letter at each dot.

R R R R

r r r

Say it aloud: **Rose** starts with the **/r/** sound.
Write the missing **R** and color the roses.

___oses

S s

Trace the uppercase and lowercase letters with your finger.

Then trace and write the letters with a pencil. Start a new letter at each dot.

S S S

s s s

Say it aloud: **Sock** starts with the **/s/** sound.
Draw a line to match each snake to its sock.

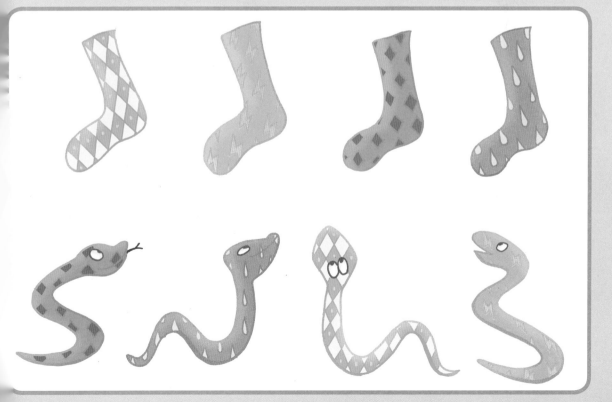

T t

Trace the uppercase and lowercase letters with your finger. Then trace and write the letters with a pencil. Start a new letter at each dot.

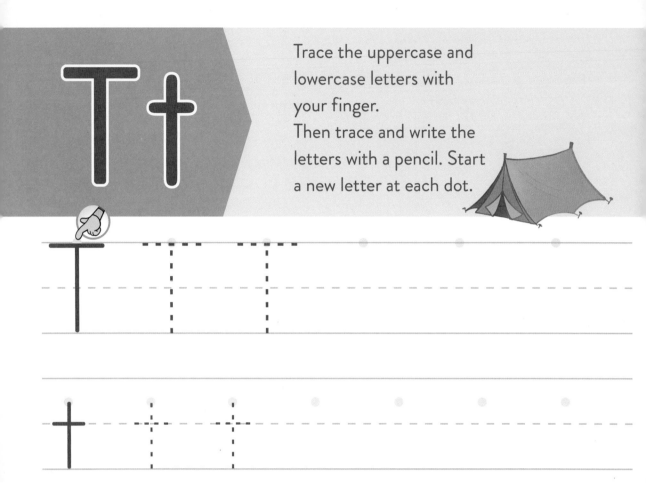

Say it aloud: **Tent** starts with the **/t/** sound. Say the name of each object aloud. Circle the objects with names that start with the **/t/** sound.

Uu

Trace the uppercase
and lowercase letters
with your finger.

Then trace and write the
letters with a pencil. Start
a new letter at each dot.

U U U U

u u u u

Say it aloud: **Umbrella** starts with the **/u/** sound.

Draw a line to lead Amelia along the path to the umbrella.

The **vowels** in the alphabet are:

A E I O U

Draw a line to match each
uppercase and lowercase vowel.

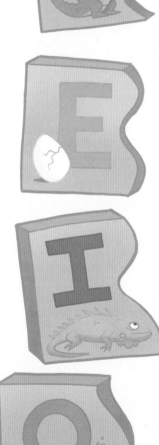

V v

Trace the uppercase
and lowercase letters
with your finger.

Then trace and write the
letters with a pencil. Start a
new letter at each dot.

V V V V

V V V

Say it aloud: **Van** starts with the **/v/** sound.
Circle each van with a **V** or **v**.

LET'S START!

GATHER THESE TOOLS AND MATERIALS.

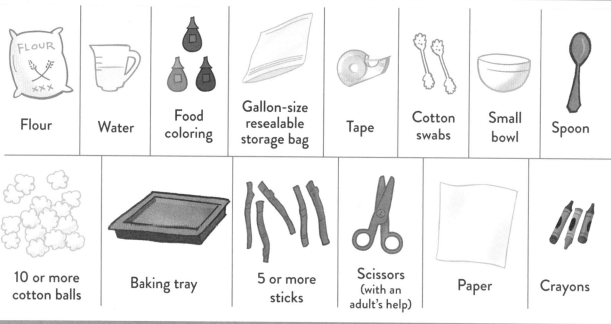

Flour	Water	Food coloring	Gallon-size resealable storage bag	Tape	Cotton swabs	Small bowl	Spoon
10 or more cotton balls	Baking tray		5 or more sticks	Scissors (with an adult's help)		Paper	Crayons

LET'S TINKER!

With the help of an adult, **combine** 1 cup of flour, 6 tablespoons of water, and a few drops of food coloring in the resealable bag.

Seal the top, and then tape the top to ensure that the bag stays closed.

Press and squeeze the plastic bag to move the contents around and mix until there are no lumps.

Lay the bag on a table and use your fingers to draw on top of the mixture.

Try drawing with a cotton swab. Which other materials could you draw with?

LET'S MAKE: COTTON BALL ROCKS!

1. With the help of an adult, **mix** ¼ cup of flour, ¼ cup of water, and 2–3 drops of food coloring in a small bowl with a spoon.

2. Dip a cotton ball into the flour paint until it is fully covered. **Place** it on a lined baking tray. **Cover** as many cotton balls as you can (about 10).

3. With the help of an adult, **bake** at 350 degrees for about 30 minutes, until the cotton ball rocks are hard. **Remove** from the oven and let them cool.

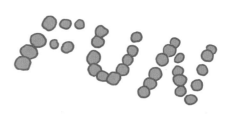

4. Take your cotton ball rocks outside. **Toss** them, smash them, and stack them. You can **make** letters, too! Can you make the first letter of your name?

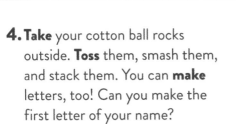

LET'S ENGINEER!

Enid is getting ready for the Tinker Town Vowel Parade!

How can she make vowel flags that everyone can see?

Gather 5 or more sticks from outside. Then **use** tape, scissors (with the help of an adult), paper, and crayons to make your own flags. How can the paper be attached to the sticks? Do your flags show the vowels uppercase, lowercase, or both? How high can you hold them? **Lead** your own Vowel Parade!

PROJECT 5: DONE!
Get your sticker!

Ww

Trace the uppercase and lowercase letters with your finger.

Then trace and write the letters with a pencil. Start a new letter at each dot.

W W W W

w w w

Say it aloud: **Worm** starts with the **/w/** sound.
Trace the lines to lead the worms to the water.

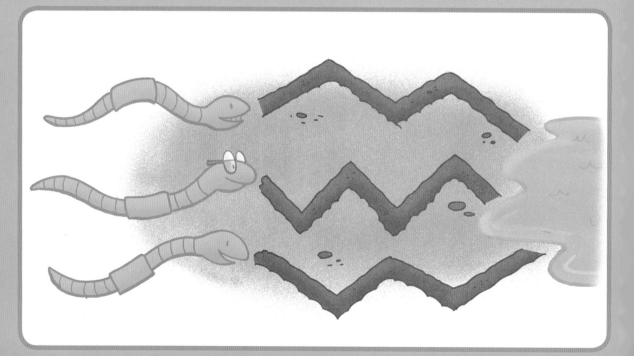

X x

Trace the uppercase and lowercase letters with your finger.

Then trace and write the letters with a pencil. Start a new letter at each dot.

Say it aloud: **Box** ends with the */x/* sound.
Circle each box with an **X** or **x**.

Yy

Trace the uppercase and lowercase letters with your finger.

Then trace and write the letters with a pencil. Start a new letter at each dot.

Y Y Y Y Y Y

y y y y y y y

Say it aloud: **Yo-yo** starts with the **/y/** sound.
Color all the yo-yos.

Trace the uppercase and lowercase letters with your finger.

Then trace and write the letters with a pencil. Start a new letter at each dot.

Z

z

Say it aloud: **Zipper** starts with the **/z/** sound.

Draw a line to move the zipper to the bottom.

Draw a line to lead Enid along the path from the ape to the zebra. Start at the letter **A**. Say the name of each letter aloud as you go.

Use the letters of the alphabet to spell your name.
Write an uppercase letter for the first letter, like this:

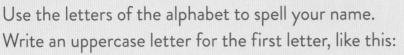

Frank

Write your name
on each item.

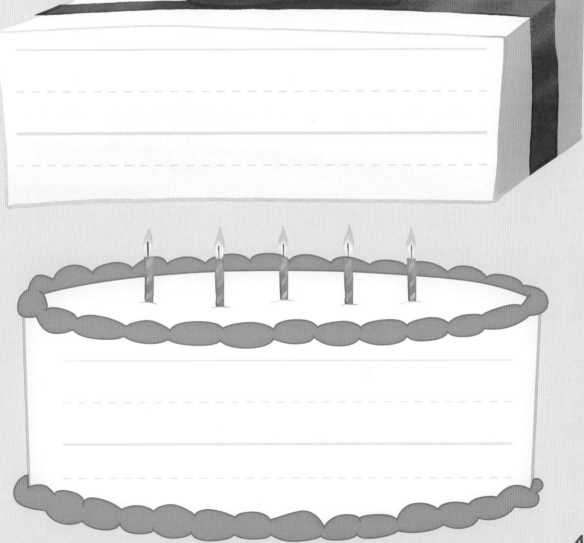

GATHER THESE TOOLS AND MATERIALS.

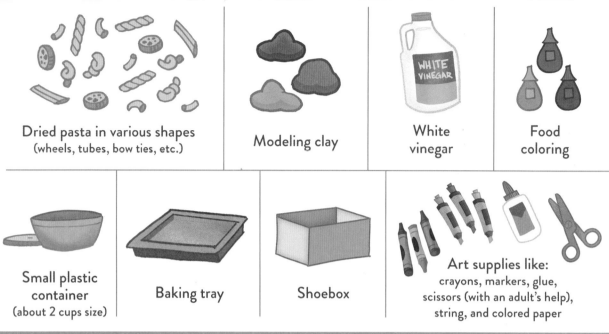

Dried pasta in various shapes
(wheels, tubes, bow ties, etc.)

Modeling clay

White
vinegar

Food
coloring

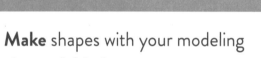

Small plastic
container
(about 2 cups size)

Baking tray

Shoebox

Art supplies like:
crayons, markers, glue,
scissors (with an adult's help),
string, and colored paper

LET'S TINKER!

Make shapes with your modeling clay and dried pasta.

Press the pasta into the clay, roll the clay around the pasta, stand the pasta up in the clay, and make sculptures. Can you make any letter shapes?

LET'S MAKE: PASTA PICTURES!

1. **Mix** 1 teaspoon of white vinegar and 2–3 drops of food coloring in a small plastic container.

2. **Add** a large handful of dried pasta to the container. **Use** as many shapes as you have—wheels, tubes, bow ties, or others!

3. Seal the container shut and shake it to mix the color and the pasta.

4. Check inside—if the pasta is covered in color, you are done. If it is not well mixed, **put** the lid back on and shake again. (You can add an extra teaspoon of vinegar to help if needed.)

5. Pour the pasta onto a baking tray and let it dry overnight.

6. Optional: **Repeat** steps 1 through 5 to make more pasta with another color.

7. When the pasta is dry, **use** it to make letters, shapes, and pictures!

LET'S ENGINEER!

*Frank is making a Name Collection. He wants to include objects that start with the first letter of his name: **F**. He already has a fish and a fork.*

How can Frank build a container for his Name Collection?

Make your own Name Collection! **Look** at your materials. **Choose** something that could hold many small objects and decorate it. Then **look** around your home to find objects that start with the same letter as your name. **Pick up** an object and say the name aloud. Then **say** your name. Are the beginning sounds the same? If so, **put** it in your container!

PROJECT 6: DONE!
Get your sticker!

Rhyming words have middle and ending sounds that are the same.

Frank's best friend MotBot loves rhyming words—even his name rhymes!
Read each pair of rhyming words and trace the middle and ending sounds.

pat a cat

hop on top

hug a bug

run for fun

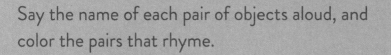

Say the name of each pair of objects aloud, and color the pairs that rhyme.

dog

log

pup

cup

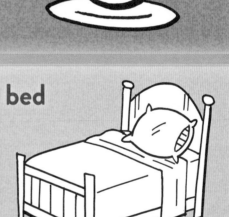

pen

bed

pig

wig

Brian's favorite letter is **B**. He likes balls and boats! Point to each picture below and say the object's name aloud. Circle the objects that start with the **/b/** sound.

Point to something you see near you that starts with the letter **B**.

Trace the first letter of each word with a pencil and read the word aloud. Then draw a line to match each word to its picture.

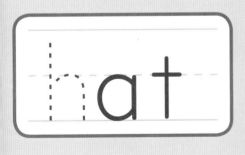

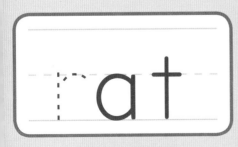

Read the letters below. Then make the sound of each letter aloud.

p f m c

Say the name of each object and listen for the sound of the first letter. Then write the correct letter to spell each word.

Read the letters below. Then make the sound of each letter aloud.

d t p h

Say the name of each object and listen for the sound of the first letter.
Then write the correct letter to spell each word.

en

en

en

en

LET'S START! GATHER THESE TOOLS AND MATERIALS.

 **Small objects like:** a penny, a cotton ball, a piece of dried pasta, a paper clip, or a pinecone

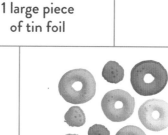 **1 large piece of tin foil**

 **10 or more pipe cleaners**

3 or more pretzel sticks

4 or more large marshmallows

A handful of cereal in various shapes

Modeling clay

LET'S TINKER!

Arrange your small objects, tin foil, and pipe cleaners to make your own robot! Which materials work best to make a body? Does your robot have arms? Or buttons? What special skills does it have? **Give** your robot a rhyming name!

LET'S MAKE: NEAT ROBOT TREAT!

1. **Push** a pretzel stick all the way through a marshmallow so that it sticks out of both ends. This is the head and antenna.

2. **Add** another marshmallow to the bottom of the pretzel. This is the body.

3. **Break** a pretzel stick in half and use the two pieces to attach 2 more marshmallows as feet.

4. Break another pretzel stick in half and add 2 arms to the body.

5. Push 2 pieces of cereal into the head to make eyes.

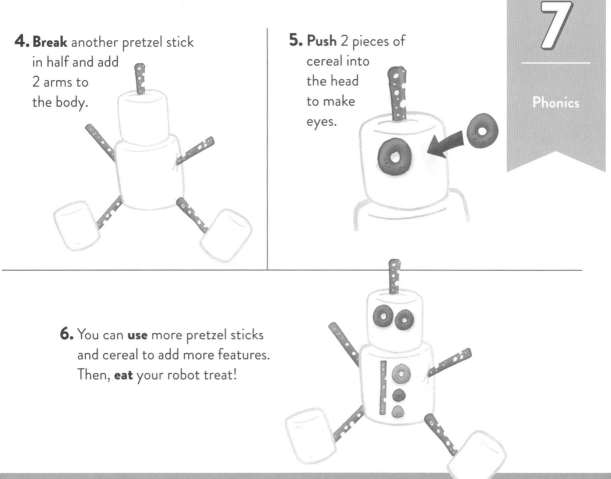

6. You can **use** more pretzel sticks and cereal to add more features. Then, **eat** your robot treat!

LET'S ENGINEER!

Frank is building a dome home for his MotBot. A dome has a rounded top, like a ball or a cave. He made a rounded shape with his pipe cleaners, but the dome keeps falling over!

How can he build a dome home for his robot that won't fall down?

Use your pipe cleaners and modeling clay to build your own dome home. How can you make a rounded top? How can the materials be used together to help it stand up? Can you make a robot to fit inside of your dome home?

PROJECT 7: DONE!
Get your sticker!

Working with Words

With the help of an adult, read the nursery rhyme aloud.

Raisin Buns

Three raisin buns in a baker's shop.
Big and round with a cherry on the top,
Along came a girl with a penny one day,
Bought a raisin bun and she took it away.

Two raisin buns in a baker's shop.
Big and round with a cherry on the top,
Along came a boy with a penny one day,
Bought a raisin bun and he took it away.

One raisin bun in a baker's shop.
Big and round with a cherry on the top,
Along came a girl with a penny one day,
Bought the raisin bun and she took it away!

You can make up more nursery rhymes about raisin buns. Start with five raisin buns and count down!

In the nursery rhyme, the words **shop** and **top** rhyme. The words **day** and **away** also rhyme. Say the name of each object aloud. On each shelf, circle the objects with names that ryhme.

Amelia sees a lot of words on her way to the bakery. With the help of an adult, point to each word and read it aloud. Then color the signs.

Draw a line to match each item to the store where Frank can buy it.

Draw a line to match each item to the store where Callie can buy it.

LET'S START! GATHER THESE TOOLS AND MATERIALS.

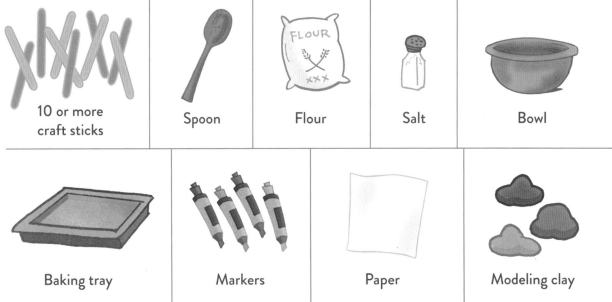

| 10 or more craft sticks | Spoon | Flour | Salt | Bowl |

| Baking tray | Markers | Paper | Modeling clay |

LET'S TINKER!

Take a craft stick and go on a word hunt. What words can you find around you?

Point to them with your stick! Which words can you read? Can you find the letters in your name?

LET'S MAKE: COLOR DICE!

1. Use a large spoon to mix ¼ cup of flour, 2 tablespoons of salt, and 2 tablespoons of warm water together in a bowl.

2. Move the dough to a table with a sprinkle of flour on it. **Knead** the dough like clay for a few minutes.

3. Form a small ball of dough into the shape of a die (a cube). **Press** your thumb into each side to make a small indent. This will help as the dough puffs up in the oven.

4. Put the dough on a baking tray. With the help of an adult, **place** the tray in a 250-degree oven for 1½–3 hours, until the dough is dry and hard.

5. When the dough is cool, **use** markers to color each side of the die a different color.

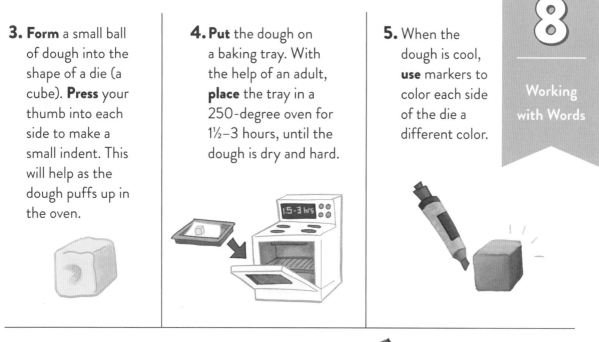

6. Find a partner to play a game! One player rolls the die and says the name of the color aloud, like red. The other player must run and touch something that is that color, like an apple. **Take turns** rolling and running.

LET'S ENGINEER!

Enid wants to buy raisin buns. But the bridge is closed for repairs!

How can she get over the lake to the bakery?

Trace your hand in the middle of a sheet of paper. **Color** it blue, like Tinker Town's lake. Using your craft sticks and modeling clay, **build** a model of a bridge that could help Enid get over the lake.

PROJECT 8: DONE!
Get your sticker!

With the help of an adult, sing this song to the tune of *"The Wheels on the Bus."*

The letters join together to spell words,

to spell words,

to spell words.

The letters join together to spell words,

We can spell anything!

What letters join together
to spell your name?

Circle each card with a letter.

Underline each card with a word.

sun

r

rain

wind

W

p

puddle

Words can be put together to make **sentences**. Words in a sentence are separated by spaces. To read sentences, follow the words from left to right.

Touch the dot under each word while you read each sentence.

Draw a line to match each MotMot to the gear they need to go outside.

To read sentences, start at the top line and move down to the bottom line. When you are done with a page, start again at the top of the next page.

Touch the dot under each word while you read these sentences.

I like red.

I like yellow.

I like green.

I like blue.

I like the rainbow!

red
yellow
green
blue

Color the rainbow.

LET'S START!

GATHER THESE TOOLS AND MATERIALS.

Small toy car (you can also use a small toy ball)	Scissors (with an adult's help)	Paper plate	5 or more sheets of different-colored paper
Glue	15 or more cotton balls	Tape	Toilet paper tube

LET'S TINKER!

Race a car from left to right, just like you read the words on a page! **Place** your car at the start of a sentence on page 70 and read. Then **look** around your home.

Can you find other sentences where you can race your car and read?

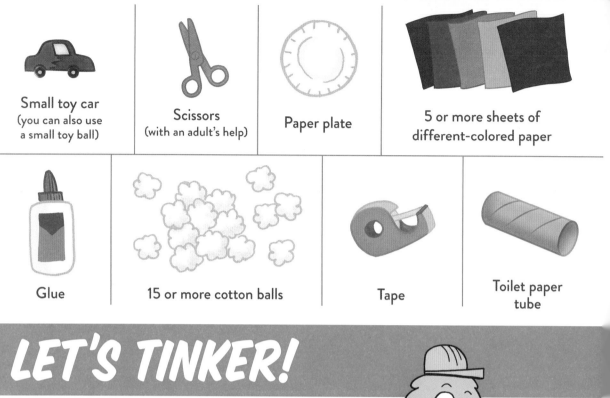

LET'S MAKE: COLORFUL RAINBOW!

1. With the help of an adult, **cut** a paper plate in half.

2. With the help of an adult, **cut** a strip from the long side on 5 different-colored sheets of paper.

3. Put a dot of glue on one end of each strip and paste them to the back of the plate at the bottom.

4. Flip the plate over and use glue to attach 15 cotton balls to the front of the plate like a cloud.

LET'S ENGINEER!

Enid is learning that letters join together to form words. Now she's noticing other things that join together to make something new: blocks stack together to make a tower. Dough, tomato sauce, and cheese join together to make pizza.

How can she put her materials together to build something new?

Use your materials to build something new—it could be a rainbow rocket or a racetrack or something completely unique! Which materials will you need? How can you hold the materials together? What colors will you use?

PROJECT 9: DONE!
Get your sticker!

With the help of an adult, read the **newspaper article** aloud.

The Tinker Town News

Fun Fun Friday

Come one, come all, to the most exciting event in Tinker Town: Fun Fun Friday. It is happening today!

In the park you'll see MotMots on the move—leaping, darting, twirling, and grooving. There are games, sports, and races. You can be big or small, quiet or loud, because everyone is welcome. And don't forget—the day ends with a dance party!

We'll see YOU at Fun Fun Friday!

Underline the **tallest** MotMot.
Then circle the **shortest** MotMot.

Quiet and **loud** are opposites. Opposites are things that are completely different from one another.

Read what each MotMot is doing. Then do the opposite and draw a picture of yourself.

Amelia is pointing **down.** Can you point **up**?

Brian is acting **sad.** Can you act **happy**?

Callie is showing an **open** hand. Can you show a **closed** hand?

Enid and Frank can't wait to dance. Draw a line to lead each MotMot through the maze to the dance party.

Join the dance party! Read each action word, and then act it out.

wiggle

bounce

hop

jump

twist

spin

Circle the move that is your favorite!

The Fun Fun Friday Opposites Game is starting. To win, the MotMots must do the **opposite** of what they are told!

Read each instruction. Color the picture of the MotMot that's doing the opposite. Then do the correct answer yourself!

Jump **far.**

Place a blanket **under** you.

Lay your socks in a **straight** line.

Look **down** and wave.

Hop on something **hard**.

Look in a mirror and **close** your eyes to see the winner of the game!

LET'S START! GATHER THESE TOOLS AND MATERIALS.

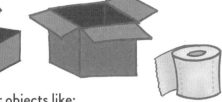

Paper objects like:
paper cups, a shoebox, a cardboard box, toilet paper

1 or more index cards
(or other small pieces of paper)

Markers or crayons

Scissors
(with an adult's help)

Tape

LET'S TINKER!

Let's move! **Create** an obstacle course. **Use** paper cups, a shoebox, a cardboard box, and toilet paper. What can you dance around? What can you jump in? What can you wiggle through?

LET'S MAKE: MOTMOTS ON THE MOVE!

1. Take an index card and draw a straight line a bit below the halfway mark.

2. On the top of the index card, **draw** the top of your favorite MotMot. You can **add** stickers from page 129.

3. With the help of an adult, **cut** two circles the size of your fingers out of the bottom.

4. Fold the card back on the line and stick your fingers through the holes. They will be the MotMot's legs!

5. Make your MotMot spin, twist, and wiggle. What else can he or she do?

LET'S ENGINEER!

It's Fun Fun Friday, and Amelia has entered the Great Tinker Town Building Game. But all the instructions are written as opposites:

- Build a **short** tower.

- Add **closed** windows.

- Raise a **small** flag.

- Make some flowers **behind** the tower.

How can she figure out what she needs to build to win the game?

Use your materials to build the opposite of each instruction! Can you create a winning tower? Which of your materials can you use to build the tower? How can you add windows, a flag, and flowers?

PROJECT 10: DONE!
Get your sticker!

Reading Comprehension

Point to each picture and tell the story
in your own words.

Circle the answer to each question.

Who is having a birthday?

What did the octopus make?

Where was the party?

Tell a family member or friend the steps that the octopus took to make the birthday treat!

Point to each picture and tell the story in your own words.

Circle the answer to each question.

Who is hungry?

What did the robot make?

Why was the rabbit happy?

Draw the food
you would order
from the robot.

Point to each picture and tell the story in your own words.

1

2

3

4

Circle the animals that hid in the tree.
Draw an **X** on the animal that was left out of the tree.

Why didn't this animal hide in the tree? Where could it go instead? Draw your own ending to the story! Then tell the story with your new ending to a friend or family member.

LET'S START!

GATHER THESE TOOLS AND MATERIALS.

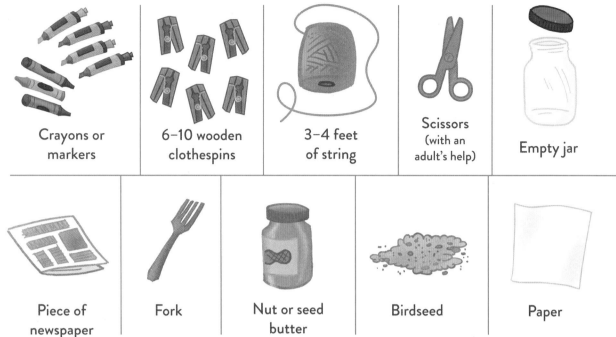

Crayons or markers	6–10 wooden clothespins	3–4 feet of string	Scissors (with an adult's help)	Empty jar
Piece of newspaper	Fork	Nut or seed butter	Birdseed	Paper

LET'S TINKER!

Use crayons or markers to draw a face on a clothespin. What other details can you add? **Clip** your new friend to your shirt. Where will you go? What will you see? **Tell** a story about your adventures!

LET'S MAKE: PICNIC FOR THE BIRDS!

1. With the help of an adult, **cut** a piece of string about as long as your body.

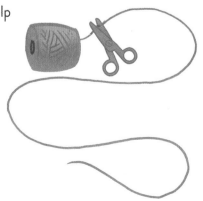

2. Tie it around the top of an empty jar, and put the lid on to hold it in place.

3. Lay a large piece of newspaper down to make a workspace.

4. Use a fork to cover the *outside* of the jar in nut or seed butter.

5. Pour 1 cup of birdseed into the middle of the newspaper. **Roll** the jar in the seeds until it is completely covered.

6. Tie the bird feeder to a tree branch outside and watch the birds come eat!

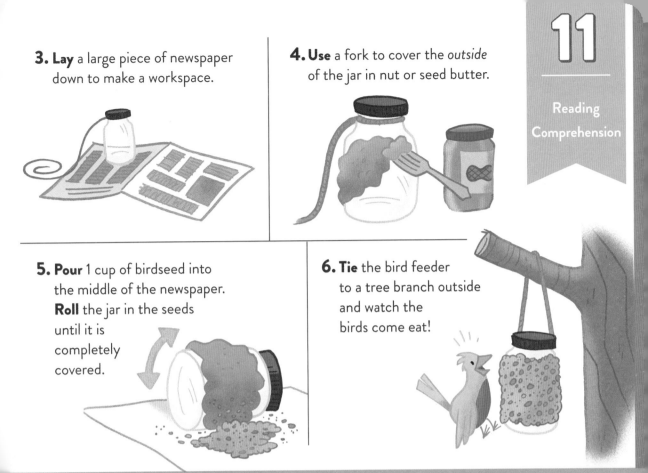

LET'S ENGINEER!

Frank loves telling stories to his friends. But his friends sometimes get confused—they can't see the story, so they don't always understand what is happening.

How can Frank show his friends what happens in his story?

Build your own people and animals to tell your own story! You can **use** paper and clothespins to make them. Then **tell** your story!
Who is in your story? What is he or she doing? Where is he or she going?
How does your story end?

PROJECT 11: DONE!
Get your sticker!

With the help of an adult, read this African folktale aloud.

The Caterpillar's Roar

A curious caterpillar saw a cozy cave and crawled inside. Later, a rabbit returned to his cave and saw some strange marks outside in the dirt. He called out, "Who's there?"

The caterpillar was worried about the loud voice outside. So she said, "Me! I am a large beast. I can stomp on an elephant!" Her voice echoed and roared inside the cave—just like a large beast! The rabbit was very afraid.

The rabbit asked his friend the leopard for help. At the cave, the leopard howled, "Who's there?" The caterpillar was worried about the howling. She said, "Me! I am a large beast. I can stomp on an elephant!" Again, her voice echoed and roared. The leopard was very afraid.

A frog hopped over to find out what was wrong. He leaped to the cave and said, "Who's there? I have strong legs and I can jump higher than an elephant!"

The caterpillar was worried about a creature that could jump so high, so she tried to sneak out of the cave. But the rabbit, the leopard, and the frog spotted her! They had been fooled by a tiny caterpillar! They laughed so hard that the caterpillar got away.

A **character** is a person or animal in a story. Cross out two pictures that were not characters in this story.

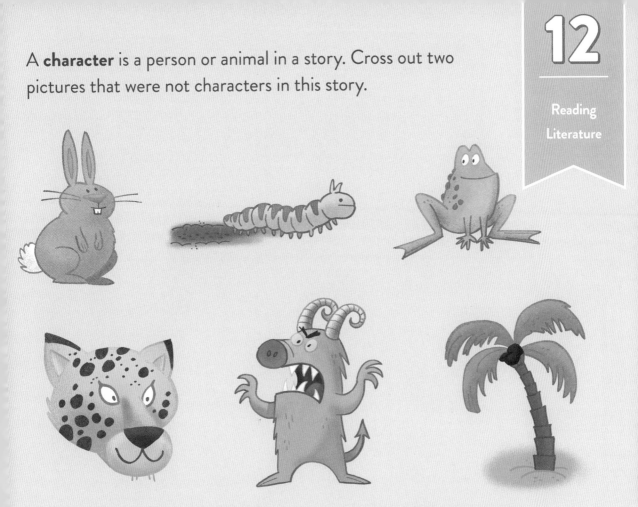

Draw a line to match the character who lives in the cave to its home.

Read the folktale again, and use a different voice for each character.

Circle the answer to each question.

Where did the rabbit live?

Who went inside the rabbit's home?

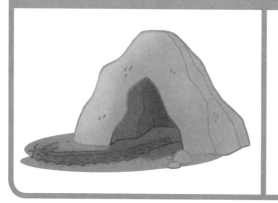

How did the rabbit know someone was inside his home?

Who was not afraid?

Share ideas with a friend or family member: **Why** wasn't this character afraid?

Point to each picture in order and retell the folktale.
Then color the characters.

1

2

3

4

5

6

In the folktale, the characters had many feelings.

The caterpillar was worried.

Draw a picture of a time that you were worried. How did you act?

The frog was surprised.

Draw a picture of a time that you were surprised. How did you act?

Read the folktale again. Talk with a family member about other feelings you hear in the story.

A **setting** is where a story takes place. This folktale takes place at the rabbit's cave.

Make your own cave with a blanket and other items around you. Then act out the story by yourself or with a friend or family member. Draw a picture of you in your setting.

LET'S START!

GATHER THESE TOOLS AND MATERIALS.

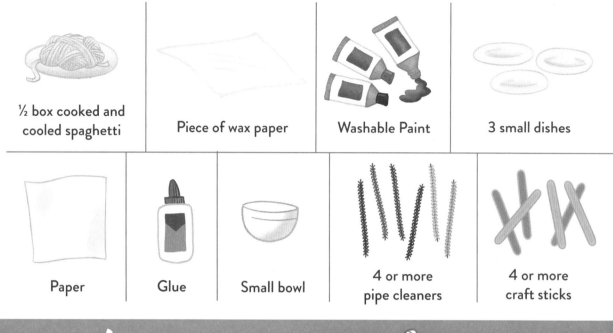

½ box cooked and cooled spaghetti	Piece of wax paper	Washable Paint	3 small dishes
Paper	Glue	Small bowl	4 or more pipe cleaners	4 or more craft sticks

LET'S TINKER!

Take a handful of cooked and cooled spaghetti noodles and place them on a piece of wax paper. **Curl** them, roll them, wiggle them, break them apart, and make pictures. What do they feel like? Can you make pictures of any characters? Can you make pictures of any settings?

LET'S MAKE: CATERPILLAR TRACKS!

1. Squeeze 3 colors of paint into 3 small dishes.

2. Drop 1 piece of cooked spaghetti into one color of paint. **Stir** it around with your fingers until it is covered.

3. pick-up the spaghetti and move it to a piece of paper. **Try** dropping it, rolling it, and dragging it to make caterpillar tracks.

4. Try again with more colors!

LET'S ENGINEER!

Amelia read a folktale about a very curious monster. The story said, "The monster lurked in the deep waters. You couldn't count its many arms and legs—they swirled all around!"

How can she build a model of the curious monster from the story?

Make a model of your own monster! **Squeeze** about a tablespoon of glue and a tablespoon of paint into the bottom of a small bowl. **Put** a handful (about a cup) of cooked and cooled spaghetti into the bowl and stir with your fingers until the spaghetti is completely covered in the colored glue. **Lift** the spaghetti out and onto a piece of wax paper. **Move** it around to create the head, body, arms, and legs of your monster. What other materials can you add to create more arms and legs? **Add** stickers of eyes and features from page 129 and let your monster dry overnight.

PROJECT 12: DONE!
Get your sticker!

With the help of an adult, read the recipe aloud.

Smiley Bread

1. Gather these ingredients: a piece of bread, nut or seed butter, a banana, and some raisins.

2. Peel the banana and, with the help of an adult, cut three slices.

3. With the help of an adult, use a knife to spread the nut or seed butter onto the bread in a circle.

4. Lay the banana slices and raisins on top to make a face.

Circle the ingredients in Smiley Bread.

Circle the tool that you need.

With the help of an adult, gather these ingredients and the tool to make Smiley Bread yourself!

Trace the numbers **1**, **2**, **3**, and **4** to put the illustrations in order from first to last. Then point to each illustration in order and retell how to make the recipe.

Amelia made her own Smiley Bread.

Find three things that are the same as Brian's and point to them.

Find three things that are different from Brian's and circle them.

Circle the pictures of other recipes Brian can make with these ingredients and tool.

Write and draw your own recipe for Smiley Bread. What ingredients will you use? What kind of face will you make?

3

Reading Informational Texts

Recipe:

_____'s

Smiley Bread

1.

2.

3.

4.

Tell a friend or a family member how to make your recipe!

TinkerActive Pre-K English Language Arts Workbook **103**

Small objects like:
a penny, a cotton ball, a piece of dried pasta, a paper clip, a pinecone, or a rock

Paper plates

Fork and spoon

English muffin

Baking tray

Small can or jar of tomato or pizza sauce

½ cup of shredded mozzarella cheese

Optional pizza toppings: pepperoni, peppers, mushrooms, or olives

Modeling clay

LET'S TINKER!

Flip, roll, stack, and line up your small materials on a paper plate. Can you make faces that are the same and faces that are different? How are they the same and different?

LET'S MAKE: ENID'S MINI PIZZAS!

1. Use a fork to split an English muffin in half.

2. Lay the 2 pieces out on a baking tray with the insides facing up.

3. Spread 1 spoonful of tomato or pizza sauce on each.

4. Sprinkle 2 spoonfuls of shredded mozzarella cheese on each pizza.

5. Add your favorite toppings, like pepperoni, cut-up peppers, mushrooms, or olives.

6. With the help of an adult, **bake** in an oven at 400 degrees for 8–10 minutes.

7. Let the pizzas cool and then enjoy!

LET'S ENGINEER!

Enid loves making her round, Enid-shaped mini pizzas. She wants to make a specially shaped pizza for her friend Frank, too.

How can Enid make a triangular, Frank-shaped pizza?

Read Enid's Mini Pizza recipe. Then **use** modeling clay to build a Frank-shaped model. (You can also ask an adult to cut an English muffin into a triangle, like Frank!)

Show your model to a friend or family member, and explain each step of the new recipe!

PROJECT 13: DONE!
Get your sticker!

Telling a Story

Frank and MotBot had an exciting day. With the help
of an adult, read MotBot's diary entry aloud.

Today I went on a robot walk with my
friend Frank. We went to the park.
We walked by a pot of flowers, a tall
slide, and a water fountain. It started
to get dark and we saw the sky turn
pink, purple, and orange! Frank
called it a "sunset." I was surprised
and excited to see it. *Beep beep*!

Have you ever seen a sunset? Tell a friend
or family member what it looked like!

Draw a line to lead MotBot through the maze to the water fountain.

Draw a picture of you with your friends. Point to each person and say his or her name aloud.

Add details by drawing the clothes each person is wearing!

Write about and draw one place you like to go with your friends.

Write about and draw one thing you like to do with your friends.

Write and draw your own diary entry about something you did with your family. Where did you go? What did you do?

Ask an adult to help you share your story! You can use computers, tablets, phones, and more.

Write about and draw how you felt. Were you happy,
excited, or nervous?

Ask a family member what he or she remembers about this event.
Write and draw the new details that you learn.

LET'S START! GATHER THESE TOOLS AND MATERIALS.

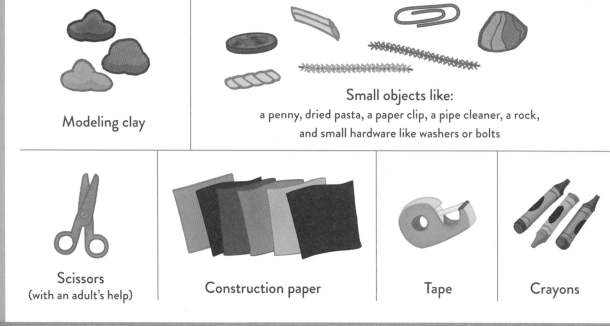

Modeling clay

Small objects like:
a penny, dried pasta, a paper clip, a pipe cleaner, a rock,
and small hardware like washers or bolts

Scissors
(with an adult's help)

Construction paper

Tape

Crayons

LET'S TINKER!

Use the modeling clay to design your own MotBot. Then **use** small objects from your materials to add details. What is it wearing? What features does it have?

LET'S MAKE: FINGER PUPPETS!

1. Cut two squares, each about 2 inches by 2 inches, from a piece of construction paper.

2. Wrap one square around your finger, like a tube, and tape it in place. Then **wrap** and tape the next one around another finger.

3. Use paper, crayons, and tape to add faces, hair, and accessories to each puppet. You can **create** your own characters or make them look like you and your family (and even your pets!). You can also **add** stickers from page 129.

4. Put the puppets on your fingers and act out your own story.

LET'S ENGINEER!

Amelia and Brian are each telling a story. Amelia's story takes place in a dark cave. Brian's story takes place on top of a volcano. They have only one ball of modeling clay to share.

*How can they build one setting that has **both** a dark cave and a high volcano?*

Use your modeling clay to build the setting for Amelia's and Brian's stories. How can you create a cave that your finger puppet can go inside? What other materials can you use? How tall can you build the volcano? What other kinds of settings can you build for your finger puppets? What stories can you tell with your characters and settings?

PROJECT 14: DONE!
Get your sticker!

Writing Informational Texts

With the help of an adult, read this article aloud.

Zebras

Zebras are amazing animals. In fact, no two zebras have stripes that are the same! So why do zebras have these unique black-and-white stripes? No one knows for sure. Many people believe that the stripes help the animals to mix together as a herd, to protect themselves from predators.

Zebras live in grasslands in Africa. There they eat leaves, twigs, and grasses. They have space to run—and they move fast. Zebras can go up to forty miles per hour. That's much faster than people can run!

Zebras are unique and interesting animals. Keep an eye out for their special stripes in pictures, at the zoo, or in Africa!

Color in the circle below each correct answer.

What colors are zebras?

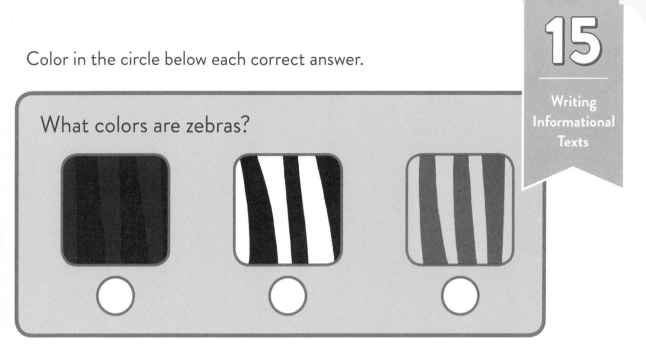

○   ○   ○

Where do zebras live?

○   ○   ○

What do zebras eat?

○   ○   ○

Write about and draw
your favorite animal.

My Favorite Animal

Point to and label any parts
of the animal that you know!

This animal lives:

on land

in the water

in the sky

○   ○   ○

This animal eats:

_____

- - - - - - - - - - - - - - - - - -

_____

This is my favorite animal because:

_____

- - - - - - - - - - - - - - - - - -

_____

Act it out: Can you move like this
animal? Does it fly, swim, or run?

Ask a friend or family member about their favorite animal.
Write about and draw what you learn.

Friend or family member's name:

Favorite animal:

What does this animal look like?

How does this animal move?

This animal lives:

on land

in the water

in the sky

○   ○   ○

This animal eats:

This is their favorite animal because:

Could their favorite animal meet your
favorite animal? What might happen?

LET'S START! GATHER THESE TOOLS AND MATERIALS.

Washable Paint	Paper	Plastic comb	Fork	Construction paper	Large paper bag
Scissors (with an adult's help)	Crayons or markers	Glue	3 large square pieces of foil		Small objects like: pennies, rocks, cotton balls, or paper clips

LET'S TINKER!

Squeeze a pile of paint into the middle of a piece of paper. **Use** a plastic comb to move the paint. What happens when you tap the comb? What happens when you drag the comb? Can you make stripes like a zebra? **Try** using a fork. How is it the same as the comb, and how is it different? **Try** again using colored paper. What colors of stripes can you make?

LET'S MAKE: ALL ABOUT ME POSTER!

1. With the help of an adult, **cut** the bottom off a paper bag.

2. Then **cut** up one long side. **Lay** the bag open flat to create a large poster.

3. Write your name at the top.

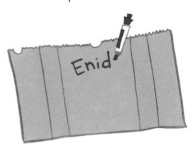

Enid

4. Draw things that mean something to YOU! You could also **cut out** pictures from magazines or photographs and glue them to the poster. **Add** your favorite things, like animals, foods, toys, and games. You could also **add** details about your life, like your family, home, and school. **Try** tracing your hand, or even your head and shoulders!

5. When you are done, **share** the poster with a friend or family member.

LET'S ENGINEER!

Callie's favorite animals are horses. She loves to play with them: She imagines that her toy horses eat grass, sleep in a barn, run, and jump!

How can she build a place for her toy horses to eat, sleep, and play?

Use foil to make models of your own favorite animals. Then **use** your materials to build a place for them to eat, sleep, and play! Do your animals need a tree? A barn? A pool? What about things to play with? When you are finished, **tell** a friend or family member what you made to help take care of your animals!

PROJECT 15: DONE!
Get your sticker!

ANSWER KEY

The Alphabet: Letters I to M

Ii

Trace the uppercase and lowercase letters with your finger. Then trace and write the letters with a pencil. Start a new letter at each dot.

I I I I I I I

i i i i i i i

Say it aloud: **Igloo** starts with the /i/ sound. Color each block with an I or i.

Jj

Trace the uppercase and lowercase letters with your finger. Then trace and write the letters with a pencil. Start a new letter at each dot.

J J J J J J J

j j j j j j j

Say it aloud: **Jelly** starts with the /j/ sound. Draw a line to connect each pair of matching letters.

Kk

Trace the uppercase and lowercase letters with your finger. Then trace and write the letters with a pencil. Start a new letter at each dot.

K K K K K K

k k k k k k

Say it aloud: **Kite** starts with the /k/ sound. Color all the kites.

Meet the MotMots!

This is Dimitri. He loves drums. Color each drum that has the letter D, like his name.

Ll

Trace the uppercase and lowercase letters with your finger. Then trace and write the letters with a pencil. Start a new letter at each dot.

L L L L L L

l l l l l l l

Say it aloud: **Leaf** starts with the /l/ sound. Say each word aloud. Circle the objects with names that start with the /l/ sound.

Mm

Trace the uppercase and lowercase letters with your finger. Then trace and write the letters with a pencil. Start a new letter at each dot.

M M M M M

m m m m m m

Say it aloud: **Map** starts with the /m/ sound. Draw a line along the path to lead Brian to the map.

The Alphabet: Letters N to Q

Nn

Trace the uppercase and lowercase letters with your finger. Then trace and write the letters with a pencil. Start a new letter at each dot.

N N N N N

n n n n n n

Say it aloud: **Nest** starts with the /n/ sound. Circle each nest.

Meet the MotMots!

This is Enid. She loves writing her name. Names begin with capital letters. Trace a capital letter E on each of her items.

NOTEBOOK Enid

Enid

Enid

Oo

Trace the uppercase and lowercase letters with your finger. Then trace and write the letters with a pencil. Start a new letter at each dot.

O O O O O

o o o o o o

Say it aloud: **Octopus** starts with the /o/ sound. Color all the octopuses.

Pp

Trace the uppercase and lowercase letters with your finger. Then trace and write the letters with a pencil. Start a new letter at each dot.

P P P P P P

p p p p p p p

Say it aloud: **Pig** starts with the /p/ sound. Say the name of each object aloud. Circle the objects with names that start with the /p/ sound.

Meet the MotMots!

This is Frank. He loves animals. Trace the missing letters to complete the name of each animal.

dog

pig

cat

fox

Qq

Trace the uppercase and lowercase letters with your finger. Then trace and write the letters with a pencil. Start a new letter at each dot.

Q Q Q Q Q Q

q q q q q q q

Say it aloud: **Quilt** starts with the /qu/ sound. Draw a line between the matching letters.

The Alphabet: Letters R to V

Rr

Trace the uppercase and lowercase letters with your finger. Then trace and write the letters with a pencil. Start a new letter at each dot.

R R R R R R

r r r r r r r

Say it aloud: **Rose** starts with the /r/ sound. Write the missing R and color the roses.

Roses

Ss

Trace the uppercase and lowercase letters with your finger. Then trace and write the letters with a pencil. Start a new letter at each dot.

S S S S S S

s s s s s s s s

Say it aloud: **Sock** starts with the /s/ sound. Draw a line to match each snake to its sock.

Tt

Trace the uppercase and lowercase letters with your finger. Then trace and write the letters with a pencil. Start a new letter at each dot.

T T T T T T

t t t t t t t

Say it aloud: **Tent** starts with the /t/ sound. Say the name of each object aloud. Circle the objects with names that start with the /t/ sound.

Uu

Trace the uppercase and lowercase letters with your finger. Then trace and write the letters with a pencil. Start a new letter at each dot.

U U U U U U

u u u u u u

Say it aloud: **Umbrella** starts with the /u/ sound. Draw a line to lead Amelia along the path to the umbrella.

The vowels in the alphabet are:

AEIOU

Draw a line to match each uppercase and lowercase vowel.

V v

Trace the uppercase and lowercase letters with your finger. Then trace and write the letters with a pencil. Start a new letter at each dot.

Say it aloud: **Van** starts with the /v/ sound. Circle each van with a **V** or **v**.

W w

Trace the uppercase and lowercase letters with your finger. Then trace and write the letters with a pencil. Start a new letter at each dot.

Say it aloud: **Worm** starts with the /w/ sound. Trace the lines to lead the worms to the water.

X x

Trace the uppercase and lowercase letters with your finger. Then trace and write the letters with a pencil. Start a new letter at each dot.

Say it aloud: **Box** ends with the /x/ sound. Circle each box with an **X** or **x**.

Y y

Trace the uppercase and lowercase letters with your finger. Then trace and write the letters with a pencil. Start a new letter at each dot.

Say it aloud: **Yo-yo** starts with the /y/ sound. Color all the yo-yos.

Z z

Trace the uppercase and lowercase letters with your finger. Then trace and write the letters with a pencil. Start a new letter at each dot.

Say it aloud: **Zipper** starts with the /z/ sound. Draw a line to move the zipper to the bottom.

Draw a line to lead Enid along the path from the ape to the zebra. Start at the letter **A**. Say the name of each letter aloud as you go.

Use the letters of the alphabet to spell your name. Write an uppercase letter for the first letter, like this:

Frank

Answers will vary.

Write your name on each item.

Answers will vary.

Answers will vary.

Rhyming words have middle and ending sounds that are the same.

Frank's best friend MuttBot loves rhyming words—even to name rhymes! Read each pair of rhyming words and trace the middle and ending sounds.

pat a cat

hop on top

hug a bug

run for fun

Say the name of each pair of objects aloud, and color the pairs that rhyme.

dog   log
Answers will vary.

pup   cup
Answers will vary.

pen   bed

pig   wig
Answers will vary.

Brian's favorite letter is **B**. He likes balls and boats! Point to each picture below and say the object's name aloud. Circle the objects that start with the /b/ sound.

Trace the first letter of each word with a pencil and say the word aloud. Then draw a line to match each word to its picture.

bat

cat

hat

rat

Point to something you see near you that starts with the letter **B**.

Read the letters below. Then make the sound of each letter aloud.

p f m c

Say the name of each object and listen for the sound of the first letter. Then write the correct letter to spell each word.

fan

pan

man

can

Read the letters below. Then make the sound of each letter aloud.

d t p h

Say the name of each object and listen for the sound of the first letter. Then write the correct letter to spell each word.

hen

pen

ten

den

With the help of an adult, read the nursery rhyme aloud.

Raisin Buns

Three raisin buns in a baker's shop.
Big and round with a cherry on the top,
Along came a girl with a penny one day,
Bought a raisin bun and took it away.

Two raisin buns in a baker's shop.
Big and round with a cherry on the top,
Along came a boy with a penny one day,
Bought a raisin bun and he took it away.

One raisin bun in a baker's shop.
Big and round with a cherry on the top,
Along came a girl with a penny one day,
Bought the raisin bun and she took it away!

You can make up more nursery rhymes about raisin buns. Start with five raisin buns and count down!

In the nursery rhyme, the words **shop** and **top** rhyme. The words **day** and **away** also rhyme. Say the name of each object aloud. On each shelf, circle the objects with names that rhyme.

Amelia sees a lot of words on her way to the bakery. With the help of an adult, point to each word and read it aloud. Then color the signs.

Answers will vary.

BUS · STOP · FLOWERS · FISH · BOOKS · BAKERY · Milk

Draw a line to match each item to the store where Frank can buy it.

Draw a line to match each item to the store where Callie can buy it.

GROCERIES · HARDWARE · TOY STORE · SHOE STORE

Reading Fundamentals

With the help of an adult, sing this song to the tune of "The Wheels on the Bus."

The letters join together to spell words,
to spell words,
to spell words.
The letters join together to spell words,
We can spell anything!

What letters join together to spell your name?

Circle each card with a letter. Underline each card with a word.

r · rain · wind · w · p · puddle · sun

Words can be put together to make **sentences**. Words in a sentence are separated by spaces. To read sentences, follow the words from left to right.

Touch the dot under each word while you read each sentence.

I like rain.

I like sun.

I like snow.

Draw a line to match each MotMot to the gear they need to go outside.

To read sentences, start at the top line and move down to the bottom line. When you are done with a page, start again at the top of the next page.

Touch the dot under each word while you read these sentences.

I like red.

I like yellow.

I like green.

I like blue.

I like the rainbow!

Color the rainbow.

Vocabulary

With the help of an adult, read the **newspaper article** aloud.

The Tinker Town News

Fun Fun Friday

Come one, come all, to the most exciting event in Tinker Town: Fun Fun Friday. It is happening today!

In the park you'll see MotMots on the move—leaping, darting, twirling, and grooving. There are games, sports, and races. You can be big or small, quiet or loud, because everyone is welcome. And don't forget—the day ends with a dance party!

We'll see YOU at Fun Fun Friday!

Underline the **tallest** MotMot. Then circle the **shortest** MotMot.

Quiet and **loud** are opposites. Opposites are things that are completely different from one another.

Read what each MotMot is doing. Then do the opposite and draw a picture of yourself.

Amelia is pointing **down**. Can you point **up**?

Answers will vary.

Brian is acting **sad**. Can you act **happy**?

Answers will vary.

Callie is showing an **open** hand. Can you show a **closed** hand?

Answers will vary.

Enid and Frank can't wait to dance. Draw a line to lead each MotMot through the maze to the dance party.

Join the dance party! Read each action word, and then act it out.

wiggle · bounce · hop · jump · twist · spin

Answers will vary.

The Fun Fun Friday Opposites Game is starting. To win, the MotMots must do the **opposite** of what they are told!

Read each instruction. Color the picture of the MotMot that's doing the opposite. Then do the correct answer yourself!

Jump **far**.

Place a blanket **under** you.

Lay your socks in a **straight** line.

Look **down** and wave.

Hop on something **hard**.

Look in a mirror and **close** your eyes to see the winner of the game!

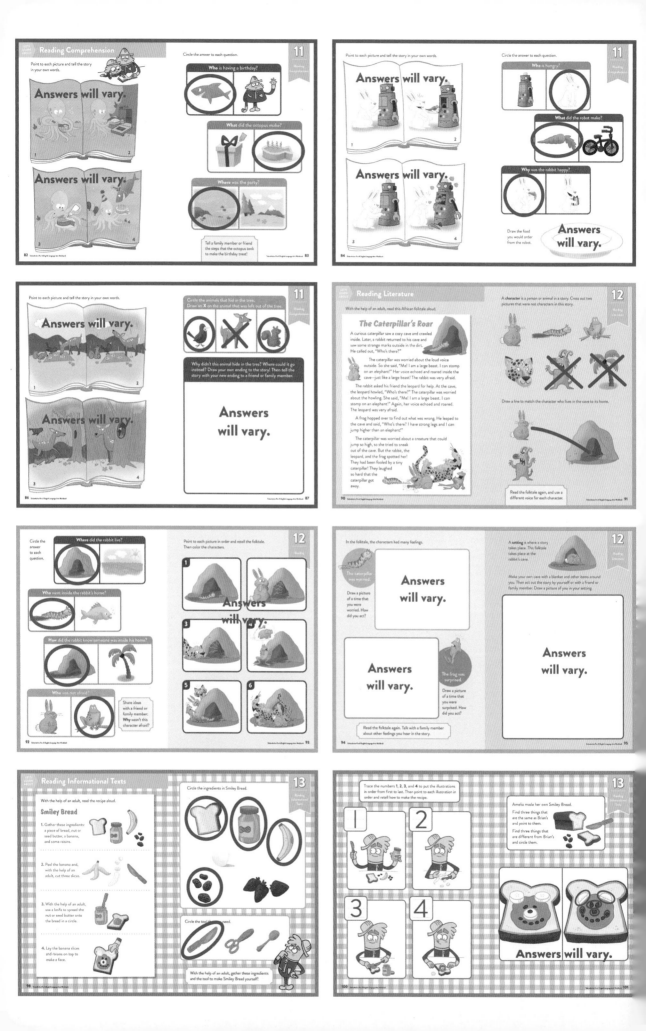

Reading Comprehension

Point to each picture and tell the story in your own words.

Answers will vary.

Answers will vary.

Circle the answer to each question.

Who is having a birthday?

What did the octopus make?

Where was the party?

Tell a family member or friend the steps that the octopus took to make the birthday treat!

Point to each picture and tell the story in your own words.

Answers will vary.

Answers will vary.

Circle the answer to each question.

Who is hungry?

What did the robot make?

Why was the rabbit happy?

Draw the food you would order from the robot.

Answers will vary.

Point to each picture and tell the story in your own words.

Answers will vary.

Answers will vary.

Circle the animals that hid in the tree. Draw an X on the animal that was left out of the tree.

Why didn't this animal hide in the tree? Where could it go instead? Draw your own ending to the story! Then tell the story with your new ending to a friend or family member.

Answers will vary.

Reading Literature

With the help of an adult, read this African folktale aloud.

The Caterpillar's Roar

A curious caterpillar saw a cozy cave and crawled inside. Later, a rabbit returned to his cave and saw some strange marks outside in the dirt. He called out, "Who's there?"

The caterpillar was worried about the loud voice outside. So she said, "Me! I am a large beast. I can stomp on an elephant!" Her voice echoed and roared inside the cave—just like a large beast! The rabbit was very afraid.

The rabbit asked his friend the leopard for help. At the cave, the leopard howled, "Who's there?" The caterpillar was worried about the howling. She said, "Me! I am a large beast. I can stomp on an elephant!" Again, her voice echoed and roared. The leopard was very afraid.

A frog hopped over to find out what was wrong. He leaped to the cave and said, "Who's there? I have strong legs and I can jump higher than an elephant!"

The caterpillar was worried about a creature that could jump so high, so she tried to sneak out of the cave. But the rabbit, the leopard, and the frog spotted her! They had been fooled by a tiny caterpillar! They laughed so hard that the caterpillar got away.

A **character** is a person or animal in a story. Cross out two pictures that were not characters in this story.

Draw a line to match the character who lives in the cave to its home.

Read the folktale again, and use a different voice for each character.

Circle the answer to each question.

Where did the rabbit live?

Who went inside the rabbit's home?

How did the rabbit know someone was inside his home?

Who was not afraid?

Share ideas with a friend or family member. Why wasn't this character afraid?

Point to each picture in order and retell the folktale. Then color the characters.

1   2   3   4   5   6

Answers will vary.

In the folktale, the characters had many feelings.

The caterpillar was worried.

Draw a picture of a time that you were worried. How did you act?

Answers will vary.

The frog was surprised.

Draw a picture of a time that you were surprised. How did you act?

Answers will vary.

Read the folktale again. Talk with a family member about other feelings you hear in the story.

A **setting** is where a story takes place. This folktale takes place at the rabbit's cave.

Make your own cave with a blanket and other items around you. Then act out the story by yourself or with a friend or family member. Draw a picture of you in your setting.

Answers will vary.

Reading Informational Texts

With the help of an adult, read the recipe aloud.

Smiley Bread

1. Gather these ingredients: a piece of bread, nut or seed butter, a banana, and some raisins.

2. Peel the banana and, with the help of an adult, cut three slices.

3. With the help of an adult, use a knife to spread the nut or seed butter onto the bread in a circle.

4. Lay the banana slices and raisins on top to make a face.

Circle the ingredients in Smiley Bread.

Circle the tool that you need.

With the help of an adult, gather these ingredients and the tool to make Smiley Bread yourself!

Trace the numbers 1, 2, 3, and 4 to put the illustrations in order from first to last. Then point to each illustration in order and retell how to make the recipe.

1   2   3   4

Amelia made her own Smiley Bread. Find three things that are the same as Brian's and point to them.

Find three things that are different from Brian's and circle them.

Answers will vary.

Page 13 — Writing Informational Texts

Circle the pictures of other recipes Brian can make with these ingredients and tool.

Write and draw your own recipe for Smiley Bread. What ingredients will you use? What kind of face will you make?

Recipe:

_____'s

Smiley Bread

1.

2.

Answers will vary.

3.

4.

Tell a friend or a family member how to make your recipe!

Page 14 — Telling a Story

Frank and MotBot had an exciting day. With the help of an adult, read MotBot's diary aloud.

Today I went on a robot walk with my friend Frank. We went to the park. We walked by a pot of flowers, a tall slide, and a water fountain. It started to get dark and we saw the sky turn pink, purple, and orange! Frank called it a "sunset." I was surprised and excited to see it. Beep beep!

Draw a line to lead MotBot through the maze to the water fountain.

Have you ever seen a sunset? Tell a friend or family member what it looked like!

Page 14

Draw a picture of you with your friends. Point to each person and say his or her name aloud.

Answers will vary.

Add details by drawing the clothes each person is wearing!

Write about and draw one place you like to go with your friends.

Answers will vary.

Write about and draw one thing you like to do with your friends.

Answers will vary.

Page 14

Write and draw your own diary entry about something you did with your family. Where did you go? What did you do?

Answers will vary.

Ask an adult to help you share your story! You can use computers, tablets, phones, and more.

Write about and draw how you felt. Were you happy, excited, or nervous?

Answers will vary.

Ask a family member what he or she remembers about this event. Write and draw the new details that you learn.

Answers will vary.

Page 15 — Writing Informational Texts

With the help of an adult, read this article aloud.

Zebras

Zebras are amazing animals. In fact, no two zebras have stripes that are the same! So why do zebras have these unique black-and-white stripes? No one knows for sure. Many people believe that the stripes help the animals to mix together as a herd, to protect themselves from predators.

Zebras live in grasslands in Africa. There they eat leaves, twigs, and grasses. They have space to run—and they move fast. Zebras can go up to forty miles per hour. That's much faster than people can run!

Zebras are unique and interesting animals. Keep an eye out for their special stripes in pictures, at the zoo, or in Africa!

Color in the circle below each correct answer.

What colors are zebras?

Where do zebras live?

What do zebras eat?

Page 15

Write about and draw your favorite animal.

My Favorite Animal

Answers will vary.

Answers will vary.

Point to and label any parts of the animal that you know!

This animal lives:

on land   in the water   in the sky

Answers will vary.

This animal eats:

Answers will vary.

This is my favorite animal because:

Answers will vary.

Act it out: Can you move like this animal? Does it fly, swim, or run?

Page 15

Ask a friend or family member about their favorite animal. Write about and draw what you learn.

Friend or family member's name:

Answers will vary.

Favorite animal:

Answers will vary.

What does this animal look like?

Answers will vary.

How does this animal move?

Answers will vary.

This animal lives:

on land   in the water   in the sky

Answers will vary.

This animal eats:

Answers will vary.

This is their favorite animal because:

Answers will vary.

Could their favorite animal meet your favorite animal? What might happen?

Odd Dot
120 Broadway
New York, NY 10271
OddDot.com

ISBN: 978-1-250-20811-8

WRITER   Megan Hewes Butler

ILLUSTRATOR   Pat Lewis

EDUCATIONAL CONSULTANT   Randi House

CHARACTER DESIGNER   Anna-Maria Jung

COVER ILLUSTRATOR   Anna-Maria Jung

LEAD SERIES DESIGNER   Carolyn Bahar

INTERIOR DESIGNER   Tim Hall

COVER DESIGNERS   Tae Won Yu

EDITORS   Nathalie Le Du and Kate Avino

Our books may be purchased in bulk for promotional, educational, or business use. Please contact your local bookseller or the Macmillan Corporate and Premium Sales Department at (800) 221-7945 ext. 5442 or by email at MacmillanSpecialMarkets@macmillan.com.

DISCLAIMER
The publisher and authors disclaim responsibility for any loss, injury, or damages that may result from a reader engaging in the activities described in this book.

TinkerActive is a trademark of Odd Dot.
Printed in China by Hung Hing Off-set Printing Co. Ltd., Heshan City, Guangdong Province
First edition, 2020

10 9 8 7 6 5 4 3 2 1

For the activity on page 33:

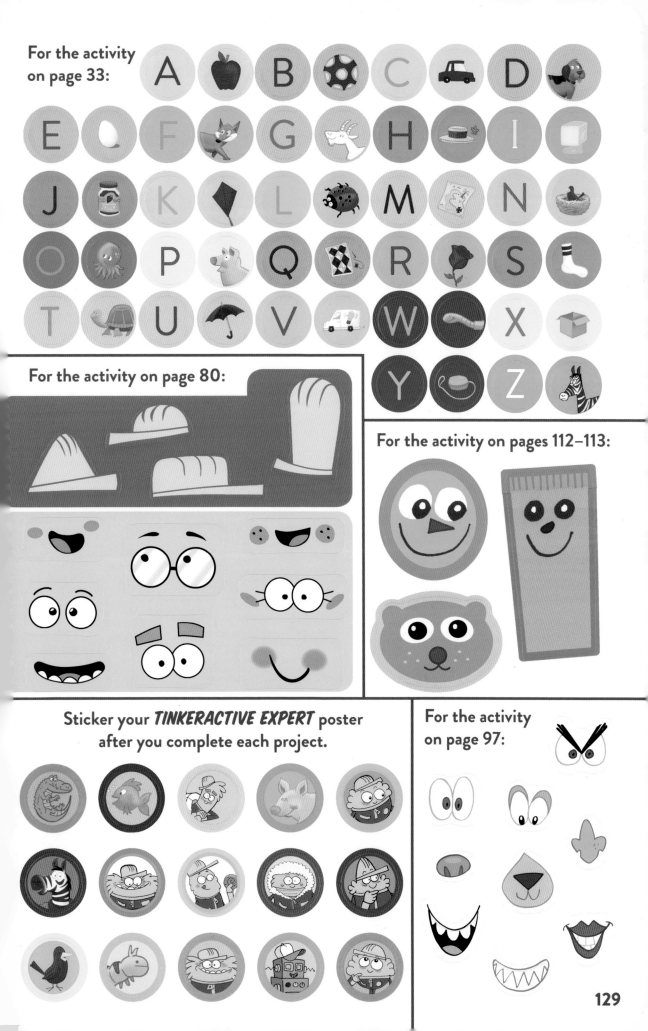

For the activity on page 80:

For the activity on pages 112–113:

Sticker your **TINKERACTIVE EXPERT** poster after you complete each project.

For the activity on page 97:

129

_____

(Your Name Here)

IS A TINKERACTIVE EXPERT!

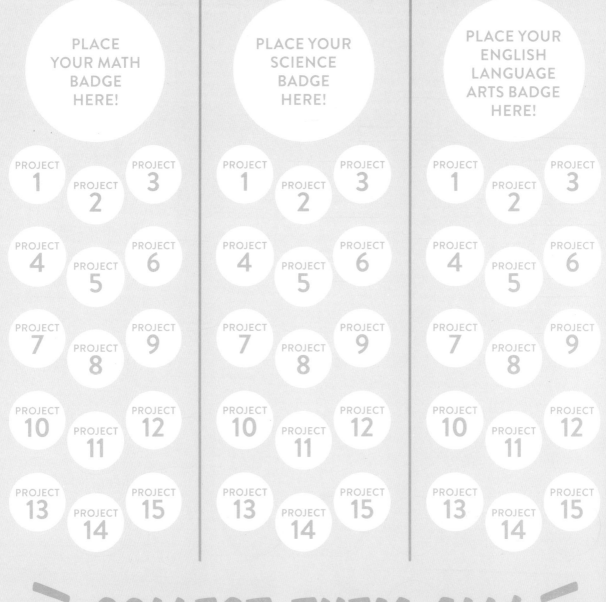

PLACE YOUR MATH BADGE HERE!

PROJECT 1 | PROJECT 2 | PROJECT 3
PROJECT 4 | PROJECT 5 | PROJECT 6
PROJECT 7 | PROJECT 8 | PROJECT 9
PROJECT 10 | PROJECT 11 | PROJECT 12
PROJECT 13 | PROJECT 14 | PROJECT 15

PLACE YOUR SCIENCE BADGE HERE!

PROJECT 1 | PROJECT 2 | PROJECT 3
PROJECT 4 | PROJECT 5 | PROJECT 6
PROJECT 7 | PROJECT 8 | PROJECT 9
PROJECT 10 | PROJECT 11 | PROJECT 12
PROJECT 13 | PROJECT 14 | PROJECT 15

PLACE YOUR ENGLISH LANGUAGE ARTS BADGE HERE!

PROJECT 1 | PROJECT 2 | PROJECT 3
PROJECT 4 | PROJECT 5 | PROJECT 6
PROJECT 7 | PROJECT 8 | PROJECT 9
PROJECT 10 | PROJECT 11 | PROJECT 12
PROJECT 13 | PROJECT 14 | PROJECT 15

= COLLECT THEM ALL! =